BRIDGING THE GAP

Bridges

Peter Ashley

Everyman Pocket Books
In association with English Heritage

Bridging the Gap – Bridges

**Published by Everyman Publishers Plc
in association with English Heritage**

© 2001 Everyman Publishers Plc
Text and photographs © Peter Ashley

ISBN 1 84159 047 9

Design by Anikst Design
Printed in Singapore

Everyman Publishers Plc
Gloucester Mansions
140a Shaftesbury Avenue
London WC2H 8HD

Berwick-on-Tweed, Northumberland
(p. 1) Three bridges over the Tweed.
Furthest away is Stephenson's 1850 Royal
Border Bridge for the railway, in the middle
the reinforced concrete road bridge opened
in 1928, and in the foreground the
sandstone bridge of 1634.
Iron Bridge, Shropshire
(p. 2) Cast by local ironmaster, Abraham
Derby, the world's first iron bridge spanned
the steeply wooded passage of the River
Severn in 1779.

contents

introduction Granite slabs rise from noisy moorland streams, intricate spiders' webs stretch across gorges, and tasteful classical details arch over parkland rivers; bridges fulfil their functions in countless ways. They may be thundered over by express trains, chugged under by canal boats, and ignored by motorway drivers. They leapfrog across meadows on stone arches, soar high over valleys on red brick piers, and swing across rivers with rumbling steel girders. Sometimes we know who built them, engineers of the calibre of a Stephenson or a Brunel, but often they're the work of unknown master craftsmen. Modest or spectacular, all are considerable achievements, born out of a pioneering spirit and inventive daring.

This pocket book follows the development of the bridge, from the first principles of utilising trees and slabs, to the high-flying concrete suspension spans of the present. It follows a rough chronology, but there are no hard and fast rules. The megalithic style of clapper bridges, for example, was still being used in the 19th century. Felmersham Bridge seamlessly takes its place in a series of medieval bridges over the Ouse in Bedfordshire, but in fact the crossing at this point only appeared in 1818. In any case, medieval bridges, like churches, have metamorphosed into what we see today through a succession of alterations over the centuries. Turvey, again over the Ouse, is typical of improvements made to take into account changes in the river, flood damage, and the widening and strengthening required to cope with the growing demands of traffic. Up to the 17th century, the heaviest load a bridge had to take was a farm wagon, and by far the most frequent users were strings of packhorses. As the building of turnpike roads increased into the 18th century, so more bridges appeared, many with toll booths or cottages. The fashion for landscaping around great country houses brought the decorative arts to new parkland bridges. The Industrial Revolution burst into fiery life with new technologies and materials, manifested in colossal achievements for the canals and railways. The bridge came to life in awe-inspiring structures, no longer restricted to narrow-arched crossings with cutwaters and refuges. Brunel staggered the world, let alone Bristol, with his aerial circus act at Clifton, and as the 19th century drew to a close, steam pumps and hydraulics bodily lifted Jones' and Barry's Tower Bridge bascules clear of the Thames. Now it's called civil engineering, but we still amaze ourselves with skywriting arcs like the superb Orwell Bridge in Suffolk, and feel the sensation of flying in our cars as we cross the Thames on the Queen Elizabeth Bridge at Dartford.

There are enough bridges in England alone to fill any number of books this size and what you will find in these pages is an idea of just how much variety there is – variety in materials, in style, and in purpose. I have found it immensely rewarding to work on a book that brings together examples as wildly different as a simple, unpretentious stone footbridge over a Cotswold stream, and an eye-popping transporter bridge across the Tees. They both provide solutions to a problem that will always be with us until we all sprout wings or drive rocket-cars.

We are all familiar with bridges, perhaps taking them for granted, but English Heritage works hard to make us aware of them. Their listing programme is saving a great many from senseless destruction or inappropriate alteration. My hope is that this little book will encourage you to take the time for a closer look, so that these delightful additions to our environment can continue to be loved and appreciated.

first principles The very first bridge, we can only assume, was an accident put to good use. A tree opportunely uprooted in some wild prehistoric storm or a slice of rock tumbling into position after a landslip sparked an idea, with stepping stones growing into clapper bridges and granite jutting out from ledges becoming cantilevers. Trees were felled deliberately, fashioned into the first beam bridges, purely to avoid lengthy detours to find a crossing. The Romans generally built in wood, and relatively complex wooden bridges constructed by the Normans survived well into the 16th century. The simplest ideas, however, are still with us – a plank over a ditch, a slab over a stream – all constantly adapted and repaired over the centuries.

Oundle, Northamptonshire A fallen tree across the Lyveden Brook

∧ **Eastleach Martin, Gloucestershire** The Cotswold River Leach divides Eastleach Turville from Eastleach Martin. Their respective churches stare at each other over the clear water. They are joined by two bridges, a double-arched 19th-century road bridge, and this sheer delight, Keble's Bridge. It is a clapper-style footbridge composed of huge slabs placed across stone piers, with steps down into the water. I sat on them for some time, pondering their use.... a convenience for laundering or baptism by total immersion came to mind.

< **Clapper Bridge, Postbridge, Dartmoor** Dartmoor has many clapper bridges, but this is the best. William Crossing's guide to the moor recalls locals speaking of the old moorland tracks as 'post roads', and a 1720 map is marked with this bridge as a 'post bridge, 3 arches'. As the turnpike roads of the late 18th century were completed, it gave its name to the settlement that arrived with them. John Lloyd Warden Page's 1889 *An exploration of Dartmoor and its antiquities* calls it the 'Cyclopean Bridge', after the architectural term for masonry using immense and irregular-shaped stones.

a succession of arches

a succession of arches Everything changed with the arch. Wedge-shaped stones or bricks, called voussoirs, are built up on a curve over a timber support, called centering. The final piece slotted home at the crown is the keystone, and the load is transferred down either side to the abutments, allowing the centering to be removed. Anonymous stonemasons developed this principle in the medieval bridge, a growing confidence resulting in increasingly ambitious structures. The piers were extended out against the river flow to form knife-edged cutwaters to reduce water pressure on the bridge, and extended upwards to form triangular-shaped refuges for foot passengers to get out of the way of wagons, animals and the occasional madman on a horse.

Anstey Packhorse Bridge, Leicestershire

Packhorse bridges are difficult to date, some being over 700 years old. They were once essential to commerce, built on trade routes to accommodate the passage of convoys of up to thirty ponies carrying twin panniers filled with goods – everything from coal and corn to pottery and lead ingots. Their width varies from two to twelve feet; many were converted for wagons and carts. Anstey is a true survivor, a late medieval specimen five feet wide and 54 feet long.

∧ **Gallox Bridge, Dunster, Somerset** The castle gathers the town around it like a hen with chickens, and the Yarn Market has bicycles propped against it and ice cream eaten in it. These are the twin trademarks of Dunster's past that everyone comes to see. Walk a little further down a lane lined with hollyhocked cottages, and behind the castle is this hidden surprise, a stone packhorse bridge the colour of Golden Syrup across the River Avill.

> **Twizell Bridge, Northumberland** An early 15th-century bridge over the wooded glen of the River Till. At ninety feet, it is possibly the largest single span medieval bridge in the country. Its high arch in pale grey stone is deeply ribbed underneath. It had a strategic role in the Battle of Flodden, as Sir Walter Scott wrote: 'The Scots beheld the English host / Leave Bardmore wood, their evening post, / And heedful watched them as they crossed / The Till, by Twizel bridge.' The gaunt ruin above it is the monster folly Twizell Castle, started by Sir Francis Blake around 1770 and never completed.

Sutton Bridge, Bedfordshire Essential repairs to this bridge between Potton and Biggleswade revealed a foundation of four elm beams felled in the 13th century. They lay across the stream bed underpinning the entire structure, the original stabilising base for the subsequent sandstone courses. A watersplash shares its crossing of the Potton Brook, a little tributary of the River Ivel.

Aylesford, Kent The Norman tower of the parish church of St. Peter and St. Paul watches over a 14th-century bridge leading into the narrow streets of this papermaking town on the Medway, a little way upstream from Maidstone. The crossing of the river here has featured in history since the locals were hammered into submission by the Jutish mercenary, Hengest, in AD 455.

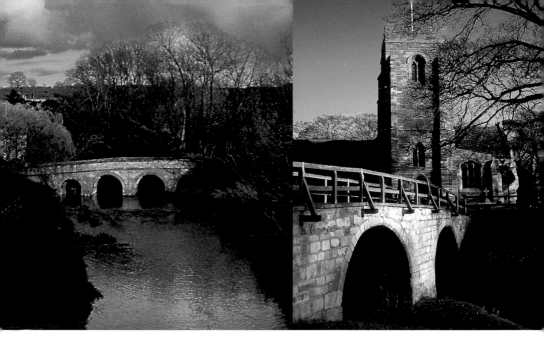

> **Duddington, Northamptonshire** Duddington is a chocolate-box Cotswold village dropped into northeast Northamptonshire. It shares the same band of oolitic limestone that joins Dorset with the coast of Yorkshire. Thought by many to be the finest looking building stone in the country, its colouring can change from grey to a fiery gold according to the light. The bridge probably originated in the 14th century, and although much altered, it still retains great charm, grouped as it is on the River Welland with a watermill of 1664 and the church of St. Mary.

> **Medbourne, Leicestershire** This medieval, three-arched bridge crosses a tiny tributary of the Welland by St. Giles church in Medbourne, Leicestershire. A little further upstream this tranquility is shattered every Easter Monday when Hallaton fights Medbourne in the annual bottle-kicking. In fact it's not a bottle, and it's more blue murder than kicking, but the objective still remains for Medbourne to get a small wooden cask filled with ale across the stream and into their parish, and for Hallaton to stop them.

Wansford-in-England, Cambridgeshire The medieval, ten-arch bridge across the Nene at Wansford once rumbled with the noise of traffic using the Great North Road. The village is now mercifully bypassed, but the Haycock Hotel is a reminder of the days when stage coaches clattered and jangled over the bridge. Here a painted sign explains the name and the addition of 'England' to 'Wansford'. In the 17th century, Drunken Barnabee fell asleep on a haycock that floated off on the flooded river, finally coming to rest against the bridge. 'Am I in Greenland?', he enquired of startled watchers. 'No, Wansford-in-England', they (probably impolitely) informed him.

Trinity Bridge, Crowland, Lincolnshire A 14th-century bridge in Lincolnshire with no water, let alone a river, in sight. This was once the crossing point of three streams where the River Welland divided, and Daniel Defoe reckoned there was a bottomless pit in the shadows of the three Ancaster stone arches. Now this strange curiosity is a meeting place and playground for Crowland's children, watched over benignly by a kingly statue that in all probability once stared out over the town from the west front of the haunting Abbey nearby.

Iford Manor, Wiltshire This is a place for river spirits, their voices murmuring in the tumbling waters of the Frome. They are no doubt listened to by the lichened stone statue of Britannia standing on the parapet of the c.1400 bridge. It was placed here by Harold Peto, a lively, funny and eccentric architect who brought a taste of Italy to this secret and lushly wooded valley to the south of Bradford-on-Avon. In the early 1900s he landscaped the garden of the early 18th-century house with terraces, loggias and sculptures, ensuring his place amongst the great English garden designers.

Before the Great Ouse finally heads for The Wash at Kings Lynn, it passes under a succession of medieval bridges of great character. Many are approached by long causeways, a testament to the extent to which the river can obliterate the road and surrounding meadows in times of floods. There is something terrifying in the sheer power of water surging past the cutwaters, leaving tiny gaps at the tops of arches, and a bewildering flood plain cutting off neighbouring villages, creating lengthy detours for motorists and rendering landscapes temporarily unrecognisable. This selection starts with Turvey and moves downstream.

Turvey An eleven-arched bridge connecting Buckinghamshire with Bedfordshire. It is an excellent example of how a bridge can be widened, as it was on the downstream side in 1930, without destroying its character. A letter to The Times in 1933 from a member of The Council for the Preservation of Rural England was very appreciative: '... even the old stones and watercourses (are) replaced in their original positions'.

Felmersham Felmersham only looks medieval; fitting perfectly into the Ouse river landscape, it was in fact built in 1818. Until then there had been no bridge on this broad loop of river that circles the village and its towering 13th-century church of St. Mary.

Bromham Bromham bridge takes the Bedford to Newport Pagnell road over the river. Until the 17th century it was known as Biddenham bridge after the village to the east. Its early history recalls a tragic incident in 1281 when 'a serious frost so injured Biddenham bridge that it gave way and a woman was carried away by the stream. She sat on an ice floe as far as Bedford bridge, when she was seen no more.'

Great Barford Parts of the original 15th-century bridge peep out from beneath a strengthening red-brick cloak added in 1874, a consequence of a traction engine falling through another county bridge at Broom. The seventeen arches are decorated with 'cog-wheel' brickwork, interspersed with black painted wrought-iron tie plates fixed to rods threaded through to the other side. These were added in 1897 by Bakers of Bedford, and when tightened they prevented the structure from bellying outwards.

Wool Bridge, Dorset Mr. Fooks' draconian warning to would-be felons on Wool Bridge over the River Frome. A gloomy cast-iron sign entirely appropriate for Thomas Hardy's Wessex.

Wilton Bridge, Ross-on-Wye, Herefordshire A splendid 16th-century announcement to this Herefordshire market town, with an 18th-century sundial in the central refuge. Appropriate to its function and position is the inscription: *Esteem thy precious time / Which pass so swift away / Prepare ye for eternity / And do not make delay.*

rooms with a view Once upon a time, a bridge was hardly finished before someone wanted to put a building on it. Usually it was a chapel built for the use of travellers, although in times of plague it would be opened for the use of sufferers, to isolate them from worshippers in the parish churches. Militarily, bridges were strategically important, and fortified bridges were crucial in the defence of castles and townships. Possibly the most famous bridge to be lived on was the old London Bridge, twenty spans of varying width supporting eclectic rows of houses and shops, complete with flying banners and traitors' heads. For 600 years it restricted the river flow, aiding the famous freezing over of the Thames, and provided sport for boatmen negotiating the sudden rush of water shooting between the arches. Its removal took with it a fashion now rarely repeated.

Bridge of Sighs, Cambridge The Bridge of Sighs connects the New and Third Courts of St. John's College. Its Venetian namesake was so-called because it led straight into a prison, although 'sighs' was undoubtedly an understatement. Pure 19th-century Gothic, the unglazed windows are crossed by iron bars to prevent students from using it as an unofficial entrance at night. As this can only be achieved from the river, they may seem superfluous.

∧ **St. Ives Chapel Bridge, Cambridgeshire** Surviving examples of bridge chapels are to be found in Wakefield, Rotherham, Bradford-on-Avon, and this example on the Ouse at St. Ives. The bridge dates from 1415, and the chapel was consecrated and dedicated to St. Lawrence in 1426. Up until 1929 this chapel had an 18th-century brick house perched precariously on top of it, but the weight was found to be slowly but surely pushing the chapel into the Ouse. On its removal, the building was restored to its original form.

< **Blenheim Palace, Oxfordshire** 'Capability' Brown's plans for the landscape at Blenheim included a need to rival the Thames, and so he set about damming the little River Glyme to form two lakes, at the same time providing an immeasurably better setting for Vanbrugh's baroque Grand Bridge. The rooms within the piers would now truly come to life, and guests could arrive by boat for the banquets laid out therein. Imagine the sound of their junketings carrying out over the calm of the lakes, with flares being lit as the bridge caught the last of the sun. On my visit, this reverie was shattered by a loud shriek mournfully emanating from one of the rooms. Not the lost soul of an over indulged, 18th-century diner, but the echoing cry of a waterfowl. Vanbrugh's original design for the bridge was topped with a roofed colonnade.

∧ **Wilton House, Wiltshire** The River Nadder gathers water from the chalk downs of Wiltshire, and just before it flows into Salisbury it finds itself amongst the lawns and cedars of Wilton House. This is the home of the Earls of Pembroke, and in 1737 the 9th Earl, known as 'the Architect Earl', built with Roger Morris this colonnaded and pavilioned bridge over the river. They had seen a drawing of Palladio's, a suggestion for the Rialto Bridge in Venice, and adapted it in a design that was so highly regarded it also ended up gracing the grounds at both Prior Park in Bath and Stowe in Buckinghamshire.

> **Lincoln High Bridge** On the left hand side of the Lincoln's High Street, as you walk up the hill, is a row of 16th-century shops and houses. Although rebuilt in 1900-01, these are the original timbers and materials. On either side are narrow steps descending to footpaths and from these the full impact is realised in a sight unique in England. The whole structure is in fact a bridge over the River Witham, with exposed timbers on the top floor and three dormer windows pointing up from the roof. The east side of the bridge once held a bridge chapel (now sadly demolished) dedicated to St. Thomas.

draughtsmen's contracts

The 17th and 18th centuries saw the emergence of architects as we now perceive them. With the dawning of the Renaissance, the Gothic stone masons who planned through to construction gave way to architects who drew up plans. The Age of Taste was born. Inigo Jones and Sir John Vanbrugh brought theatrical designs to life on the country estates of wealthy patrons. The landscaping of 'Capability' Brown dotted with Robert Adam's garden caprices brought Arcadia to Essex. The bridge became a work of art as classical balustrades formed parapets and Roman river gods in alcoves took up sentry duty. Parchment plans with the ink barely dry were thrust into the hands of masons at universities, and turnpike engineers built for the golden age of the stage coach.

Tyringham Bridge, Buckinghamshire Tyringham House was designed by Sir John Soane in the late 18th century, but sadly and ruthlessly altered in 1909. Two survivors of his vision are the entrance gate on the Northampton to Newport Pagnell road, and this handsome bridge over the Great Ouse. Both have Soane's signature of finely incised lines and round-headed alcoves, and the isolated parkland setting of the bridge is perfect for appreciating the high sweeping hump of the single arch.

∧ **Greta Bridge, Durham** Here is the inn where the coach deposited Nicholas Nickleby, Wackford Squeers and a collection of small boys with all their 'united luggage'. Charles Dickens' 'Dotheboys Hall' was still three miles distant. Greta Bridge is no longer subject to heavy traffic, as the A66 now slices through Rokeby Park, leaving this elegant 18th-century arch in peace as it spans the River Greta. It was designed by John Carr of York in 1793.

› **Lilford Bridge, Northamptonshire** This is deeply wooded country south of Oundle in Northamptonshire. Here the River Nene is more likely to be heard than seen, with thundering locks and weirs amongst the trees by the Lilford estate. Lilford Bridge comes as a delightful surprise after a bend in the lane as it arrives at the river. Built in 1796, the single arch is crowned by balustrades of creamy Weldon stone. The eastern parapet has recently been sensitively restored to its former glory after an over zealous driver toppled its entire length into the river. Divers carried out a fingertip search for the stone in nine feet of gloomy pike-haunted water.

Clumber Bridge, Nottinghamshire A series of trumpeting gates and lodges circle the vast estate of Clumber. From the finest, the Apleyhead Gate, a three mile avenue of four rows of lime trees runs through the park. One expects at any moment that a house worthy of these announcements will appear through the oaks and cedars. Sadly, it was destroyed before the war, leaving only the stunning 1889 chapel to mourn its passing. The best view of its tower and spire soaring up from the lake is from Stephen Wright's 18th-century, three-arched bridge over the River Poulter. The slightly eerie atmosphere may well be defined by a spectral heron launching off from the balustrades.

Godmanchester, Cambridgeshire Before the Great Ouse slowly winds past Huntingdon, it divides to form islands to the west of Godmanchester. (John Betjeman encouraged his children to pronounce it 'Gumster'.) These flat fields lined with willows, known as Port Holme, are reached from the town by the wooden Chinese Bridge. Quite why 'Chinese' it's difficult to say, except for the fact of its chequered and puzzling history. Designed in 1827 by a J. Gallier, it was rebuilt in 1869, only to be replaced with a replica in 1960 and restored again nineteen years later. This part of the river is the Mill Pond, and the buildings flanking the bridge are the old Town Hall and the red brick Queen Elizabeth Grammar School.

Lion Bridge, Alnwick, Northumberland Passengers in coaches on the Great North Road would once have drawn level with this lead lion, his ramrod tail pointing back to Alnwick and the castle on the hill over his right shoulder. He stands on the eastern parapet of John Adam's 1773 Lion Bridge, the emblem of the Percy family who have resided here since 1390. The bridge itself is baronial Gothic, with its battlements and lookouts high above the River Aln.

Honington, Warwickshire To the north of Shipston is a turning for Honington marked with gate piers topped with pineapples. The lane arrives in park-like country and crosses the Stour on this classical bridge with honey-coloured stone balls marking the parapet. The gate piers and bridge are strong clues to what lies ahead in the village: a 17th-century house built by London merchant Henry Parker, and down a drive dark with yews, an equally classical church. Here the marble figures of Parker and his son stare out at box pews from under funerary swags and urns.

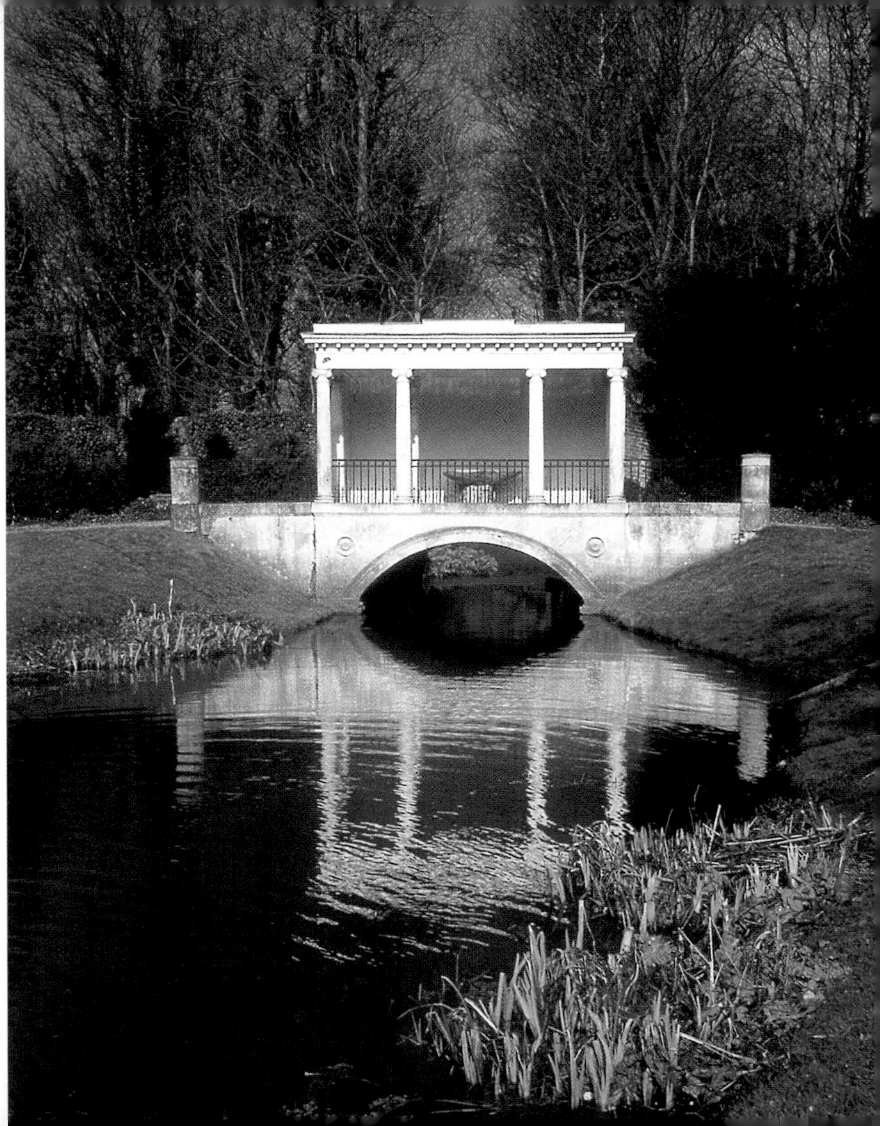

Audley End, Essex 'Too big for a king, but will do well for a Lord Treasurer' was the sarcastic comment of James I on seeing the magnificent house built by the Earl of Suffolk. One of the most significant of Jacobean houses, Audley End still reveals the tastes of succeeding generations who have left their mark on the house and its landscape. The late 18th century saw the parkland transformed by Lancelot 'Capability' Brown, and the arrival of two bridges by Robert Adam.

∧ The first was the balustraded three-arched bridge over the Cam, lying to the southwest of the house on the road that leads up to the Lion Gate and Saffron Walden. A good place to watch the ducks and peacocks lording it in the park.

< Away amongst the trees to the north is Adam's delightfully evocative 'Teahouse' bridge, a Palladian summer house of 1783. It only needs a trick of the light to see ladies moving silently towards it from the house, parasols twirling, dresses swishing across the grass.

collection points The improvement of roads required money. At first, tolls were extracted from travellers but there was nothing to bar their way, a situation which was liberally taken advantage of. The first barriers were pikestaffs, tilted up to allow traffic through, hence 'turnpikes'. Bridges were no exception, their construction often privately paid for, with tolls taken by the owners. In the late 18th century, 10d for every score of oxen was good money. The right to exact payment for a crossing has in many cases been passed down from generation to generation. Toll bridges are now rare, but as on many of our major roads, their past is still evident in surviving toll keepers' cottages.

Cookham, Berkshire A blue arch of cast iron across the Thames, curving down to a red pepperpot tollhouse on the Buckinghamshire bank. This 1867 bridge has the look of a Victorian seaside pier, with its spindly iron legs and maritime colouring. It was cast by Pease Hutchinson at their Skerne Iron Works in Darlington. This is the bridge whose pierced quatrefoiled parapet forms the background of Stanley Spencer's painting, *Swan Upping at Cookham.*

ᵛ **Eynsham, Oxfordshire** Here the River Thames braces itself for Oxford, passing under the Swinford toll bridge just outside of Eynsham. It was built by the Earl of Abingdon in 1777 as part of a new turnpike road. The tollhouse appears to be a one-storey cottage at road level, but a walk down to the riverside reveals it to be the top storey of a tall riverside house. The toll collector now stands issuing multi-coloured tickets from a tiny glass booth in the middle of the road, not so much to weary travellers on horseback these days, but more likely to excitable men in red Alfa Romeos taking the short cut to Oxford.

> **Whitney-on-Wye, Herefordshire** A tariff board on the white cottage tells us that in Georgian times a dog pulling a cart would be charged 2d to use this toll bridge over the River Wye. Between Hereford and Brecon it provides an alternative route to Hay-on-Wye. Dog-pulled carts are somewhat rare now, but tolls are still exacted from anyone wishing to trundle over the wooden decking.

SWINFORD TOLL BRIDGE

TOLLS

MOTORCYCLE (WITH OR WITHOUT SIDECAR)
CARS
TRAILER/CARAVAN   } 5
MINIBUS (MAXIMUM 16 PASSENGERS)
GOODS VEHICLES WITH TWO (2) AXLES

SINGLE DECK BUSES   12 P
DOUBLE DECK BUSES   20 P

VEHICLES WITH MORE THAN TWO (2) AXLES 10

By Order of the DEPARTMENT OF TRANSP
With Effect from 27TH NOVEMBER 1994

down on the cut

The Industrial Revolution gained momentum with an insatiable appetite for raw materials, and the new manufactured goods required faster and more efficient ways to get to their markets. Transport by river was improved by widening, deepening and straightening the water courses – the first steps towards purpose-built canals. The first totally man-made inland waterway was the Bridgewater Canal opened from Worsley to Manchester in 1761, engineered by the millwright James Brindley. Canal mania gripped the country, and canals meant bridges. Wherever the new navigations were cut, landowners needed crossings to link their divided fields. Canal companies developed a variety of individual styles, but the most ubiquitous remained the single-arched, brick 'accommodation' bridge.

Sutton Stop, Hawkesbury, Warwickshire All but engulfed by the environs of Coventry are the calming waters of the Sutton Stop. Named after the original toll keeper, this is the meeting of the Oxford and Coventry canals. They were both engineered by James Brindley to serve the coalfields of North Warwickshire. The undoubted star is this grade II listed, cast-iron towpath bridge over the actual junction. Engineered by J. Sinclair, it was cast in Derby's Britannia Foundry in 1837.

Bridge 30, Grand Union Canal, Northamptonshire A typical red brick accommodation bridge on the Grand Union near Stanford-on-Avon. Built in the last years of the 18th century, these simple country bridges were built wherever footpaths, animals or farm equipment needed to cross the canal. The canal narrowed under these bridges to save money, the tight fit becoming known as the 'bridge hole'.

Cosgrove, Northamptonshire The Grand Junction Canal starts in Braunston near Rugby and Brentford in Middlesex. The two halves meet here on the Northamptonshire–Buckinghamshire border at Cosgrove. A cul-de-sac in the village crosses this c.1800 bridge, the sort of thing you'd expect to find in the park of a country house. Very Gothick and very grand for a canal.

< **Lift Bridges** A taste of Holland where Shropshire drifts into Wales. Out in the fields near Whixall is this counter-weighted lift bridge, one of a series on the Llangollen Canal. The bridge was closed and fenced off to the lane on my visit, and just to make sure, they'd removed the roadway section for good measure. I include it because it still represents how the canal environment is considerably enhanced by these graceful structures. The line of the canal can be seen across the fields as the white balancing arms stretch up over the hedgerows.

∧ The Shropshire Union at Wrenbury in Cheshire, and the bridge is busy. When a key is placed in the control box, lights flash and a barrier can be placed over the road. The chains then tighten and pull up the drawbridge.

stories of suspense Ever since early man swung between trees on the end of a vine, we've had the principle of the suspension bridge, and we can muse on its efficiency every time we swing in a hammock (assuming it's securely tied). They are the only bridge type that openly show their means of support, a skeleton of chains and cables slung between pylons. The principle has stretched over time, from Tarzan jungle antics on vines and rope bridges, through the casting of massive links that can expand up to twenty inches in hot weather (Clifton), to the aerial acrobatics of immense spans across estuarine landscapes.

Marlow, Buckinghamshire Marlow's elegant suspension bridge was built by William Tierney Clark in 1832, the same year as C.F. Inwood's parish church. Clark originally worked at the Coalbrookdale Ironworks where the world's first iron bridge was cast, and he designed the first Hammersmith Bridge. The acclaim for his Marlow design was such that he was commissioned to build the suspension bridge across the Danube in Budapest.

∧ **Horncliffe Union Bridge, Northumberland** Little signs saying 'Chain Bridge' point down narrow lanes to the earliest surviving iron suspension bridge in Europe. A wholly unexpected sight through the trees, two pink stone pylons suspend the roadway from wrought-iron links patented by the bridge's designer, Sir Samuel Brown, three years before its opening in 1820. The pylon on the Scottish bank of the Tweed is arched and once served as a tollhouse, the other on the English side is formed in the cliff face.

< **Queen Elizabeth II Bridge, Dartford, Kent** On 30th October 1991, the third crossing of the Thames between Dartford and Thurrock was opened. The other two are road tunnels, stretched to their limits on the completion of the M25. Most people's view of it will be travelling southbound from Essex into Kent, a few seconds' aerial view of the Thames with a power station, oil storage tanks and ocean-going container ships waiting at jetties. A walk along a deserted riverside footpath from Greenhithe brings all the dizzying statistics to life: 145,000 cubic metres of concrete, 19,054 tonnes of structural steel, 750,000 high strength bolts, and 112 cables weighing 15 tonnes each. The pylons soar upwards for 137 metres above the river, and the paint order was for 48,800 gallons. The cost: £86 million to build it, £1 to cross it.

^ **Clifton, Bristol** In Brunel's lifetime all he saw of his creation were the pylons and a bucket on a cable that Bristol folk would pay five shillings to ride in, back and forth 250 feet above the Avon Gorge. In 1864 it was finally completed, although without the sphinxes that Brunel had designed to lie on the towers. John Betjeman described it in his *English Cities & Small Towns* as ' ...a delicate balanced structure, like an insect of enormous size pausing astride the rocks and trees'.

In the mind there are perhaps two Clifton bridges. One is the bridge that seems to join two woods in the sky, Betjeman's insect always drawing the eye upwards from the river and the road to Avonmouth. Then there is the sight of the two stone Egyptian pylons emerging from the downland trees in Clifton. A sign with the telephone number for the Samaritans is the first clue that a yawning chasm is about to open up under the airy suspension cables. They say that the only known survivor of a death-wish leap was a Victorian lady whose crinoline parachuted her down to the water.

Humber Bridge, East Riding of Yorkshire & North Lincolnshire Because of the political expediency often quoted as the reason for this magnificent bridge's existence, it is sometimes cruelly referred to as the 'bridge from nowhere to nowhere'. Nothing could be further from the truth. Coming down from the sweeping Lincolnshire Wolds, the road rises to fly over the broad expanse of the River Humber and down again into East Yorkshire, connecting Barton-on-Humber with Hessle, the posh west end of Hull. At around 1,480 yards, this is the world's longest suspension span and the first to make use of reinforced concrete towers. Opened in 1981, this aerial experience takes place 520 feet above the river at high water. This view is from the northern Hessle foreshore, complete with the poet Philip Larkin's 'gull-marked' mud.

heavy duties

Victorian England, and bridges had even greater demands placed upon them. One was the increased capability needed to support heavier loads, another the requirement to physically move the bridge itself. The railway age steamed in with locomotives and rolling stock on tentacles of track reaching into every community. These new iron roads had to overcome many obstacles, from country lanes and streams to river valleys and estuaries. Sometimes it was straightforward, and an unpretentious latticed girder bridge or simple brick arch sufficed. Often the problem meant leaps of faith into the unknown, and landscapes were changed beyond recognition with giant viaducts over entire valleys. This was the age of the engineering heroes. Their skills were further tested by the need for unimpeded passage for shipping, particularly in low level locations. So bridges themselves gained movable parts, lowering, raising, swinging their spans, making way for trawlers in Whitby, coasters to Wisbech, and clippers on the Tees.

Welland Valley Viaduct, **Northamptonshire & Rutland** Outside of London, this is the longest viaduct in Britain. Locally it is named either after Seaton, to the north in Rutland, or Harringworth to the southeast in Northamptonshire; apocryphally the name is decided each year by a tug-of-war between the two villages. But for everyone else it's the Welland Valley Viaduct, named after the river that marks the county boundary. It is 1,275 yards long, with 82 brick arches costing £1,000 each in 1879, and built on waterlogged fields drained by the simple expedient of laying down over one million sheepskins.

Digswell Viaduct, Welwyn, Hertfordshire Goal posts 100-feet high in the Mimram valley. It is a superb monument to the work of Sir William and Joseph Cubitt and Thomas Brassey, the contractor. The typically severe Great Northern style of 1850 contains thirteen million bricks in its forty arches. From a passenger train it can go virtually unnoticed, from below it is inspiring.

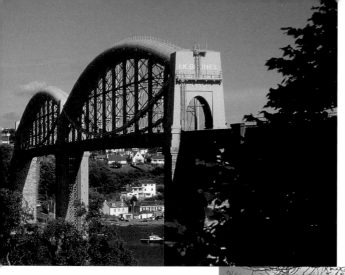

Great Torrington Aqueduct, Devon 'Tarka drifted under the high lime-spiky arches of the bridge, and the white owl, roosting on a ledge below the parapet, beside the briars of a dog-rose growing there with hawkweeds, saw him going downstream.' This is the Canal Bridge of Henry Williamson's *Tarka the Otter*, engineered by James Green for Lord Rolle's canal in 1824. The canal carried agricultural lime from Rolle's kilns down to Bideford for shipping, but now the lime-streaked aqueduct is part of the driveway to Beam House.

Royal Albert Bridge, Saltash, Cornwall When the railway arrived in Plymouth, it paused for breath before taking on the 1,100-foot crossing of the Tamar into Cornwall at Saltash, to which the Admiralty had added a demand for a 100-foot headway for its ships. Although named after the Prince Consort, and opened by him two years before his death, it is a lasting memorial to the inimitable engineering skills of the stovepipe hatted, cigar smoking Brunel; his name is emblazoned on the portals at either end. This is the only railway carrying suspension bridge in the world, the deck for the track suspended from two enormous wrought-iron tubes. After its opening in 1859, the seriously ill Brunel was able to inspect his construction lying in an open-topped carriage.

> **Cross Keys Bridge, Lincolnshire** The
River Nene is almost at its outfall into
The Wash at Sutton Bridge. The third
19th-century structure to span the river,
the hydraulically powered Cross Keys
swing bridge was built by A. Handyside
& Co. of Derby in 1894-97. Originally
carrying both road and railway between
Norfolk and Lincolnshire, the entire
shuddering mass of bowstring-braced
girders moves to give shipping access
to Wisbech. A sign on the west bank
delivers the surreal message: 'Please
dip headlights as ships approach'.

>> **High Level Bridge, Newcastle-upon-
Tyne** Robert Stephenson's High Level
Bridge carries both road and rail traffic on
its two-level structure. Bowstring girders
carry three tracks 120 feet above the
Tyne. Stephenson superintended the
driving of the first pile, and it was opened
by Queen Victoria in 1849. Behind it can
be seen the classic arch of the road
bridge and the shallower curve of a swing
bridge topped with its operating tower.

Middlesbrough Transporter Bridge A strange leviathan astride the Tees, a bridge so defining of Middlesbrough that it appears as the council logo. This is a transporter bridge, the only working example in England (there is another of differing design in Newport in Wales). The principle is beautiful because it's so simple. A normal bridge in this location could not, certainly in 1911, give the required headroom for tall masted ships, so two towers 160 feet above river level support a 571-foot span. From this is suspended a yellow gondola on bare trolley wires that can carry nine vehicles from Middlesbrough to the opposite shore at Port Clarence, in two minutes. And then it repeats the journey back again. It has remarkably survived not only these rationalising times, but also aerial attacks by both a Zeppelin and the Luftwaffe. Long may it rumble so purposefully across the Tees.

london pride The technology in place, the Victorians did what came naturally – disguise. A bridge could become a civic statement, a device combining engineering with overt decoration. As the age progressed, towns and cities needed buildings that reflected the pride in their new wealth. None more so than in London, where bridges became perfect canvases on which to apply the icons of civic confidence. A kit bag of Gothic references was shaken out and put into service.

Archway, Highgate To those travelling along Hornsey Lane, this bridge appears as if it is about to cross a railway line instead of a ravine in which red buses pass up and down from the domes and towers of the city. Viewed from underneath as one climbs the Great North Road to Highgate, it has a slightly sinister air and for me it never fails to produce a shudder as I pass under the cast-iron spandrels and railings. Alexander Binnie's 1897 high flyer replaced the original built by Nash in 1812 as an alternative route to avoid Highgate Hill.

Tower Bridge, Southwark London's trademark bridge, emblazoned and caricatured on everything from restaurant plates to souvenir leather bookmarks. Standing as a gateway to the City, it first raised its drawbridges in 1894, a Gothic fairy tale designed by Sir Horace Jones to chime with the Tower of London next door. The engineer was Sir John Wolfe Barry, and the roadways were originally lifted by hydraulic power provided by the magnificent Armstrong Mitchell steam pumps that are carefully preserved in the engine house under the southern approach. The towers contain lifts up to the overhead walkway, 142 feet above high water.

Stories of the bridge have now been told for over 100 years, but two in particular uniquely capture the imagination. Christmas 1935 saw the drawbridges start to open as a No.78 bus was already at the point of no return. The driver accelerated and leapt across the widening gap. A medal was pinned on his uniform, and £10 given from public funds. This circus act was probably watched by the pigeons who favour the underside of the drawbridges. They build nests with ergonomic care so that their young remain secure even when the opening bascules are at a dizzying angle of eighty degrees.

Albert Bridge, Battersea Ian Nairn, in his superbly individual *Nairn's London* describes the Albert suspension bridge as '...absurdly over-spiky and over-strutted'. Exactly. The pylons, in pistachio and seaside shades of blue, radiate wrought-iron stays in all directions, with the parapets and stairways finished in salmon pink and pale mustard. The whole confection is lit at night by what looks remarkably like plain household light bulbs. Another memorial to the name of the Prince Consort who had died ten years earlier, Rowland Mason Ordish designed the bridge around his rigid suspension principle in 1871. After the Second World War the LCC was seized by the desire to pull it all down, but thought again when confronted by John Betjeman leading the population of Chelsea.

Hammersmith Bridge A green and gold giant, Bazalgette's bridge of 1883-87 has an undoubted mission to impress with an exuberant display of massive detail. The towers are clad in cast iron, gilt lining taking the eye up to the fishscale roofs of the French-style pavilion tops. The steel eyebar chains are anchored in abutments stamped with badges so large you need to be in the mansion flats opposite to fully appreciate them. Every device is brought out of the catalogue of heraldic devices: castles and portcullises, horses, lions and crowns, all encircled with gilded oak leaves.

set in concrete The Romans were used to it, but it wasn't until the 20th century that concrete found new and exciting expression. After the First World War, it was reinforced with steel, and its properties became that of an artificial stone. The timber shortage in postwar Britain gave it new opportunities in the flood of rebuilding, and prefabricating brought great savings in costs and time. Pre-stressing brought a quality of lightness and an improved weight-stress ratio, ideal for shaping arches and precision jointing, properties ideal for the new generation of elegant bridge building. Berwick-on-Tweed's replacement for the 1634 sandstone bridge (see page 1) was a record for reinforced concrete (a length of 1,400 feet in 1928) but the material was still used to emulate stone. It needed the later massive civil engineering projects to enable concrete to flex its muscles, the eccentric Kingsferry Bridge over the Swale and the skyscraping Orwell Bridge leading the pack of hundreds of motorway and arterial road bridges.

North Muskham, Nottinghamshire Many of these overlooked concrete bridges are now being considered for listing. Here's one that's made it, carrying a minor road over the A1 just north of Newark.

> **Kingsferry Bridge, Kent** Early morning on the River Swale. These landmark hoops mark the passage from 'mainland' Kent onto the Isle of Sheppey. Here, both the railway to Sheerness and the A429 from Sittingbourne are lifted horizontally between the giant towers to allow shipping on the Swale in and out of Ridham dock.

∨ **Orwell Bridge, Suffolk** Traffic anxious to get to the Suffolk coast will soar over the River Orwell on this spectacular arch, but it's worth a detour onto the Shotley peninsula to see it from ground level. Modern bridges don't normally inspire affection, but this one has found a deserved place in the hearts of East Anglians, and none more so than in the little red brick cottage that snuggles up to it at Wherstead. The engineers were Sir William Halcrow & Partners, and it was opened much to the relief of the town of Ipswich in 1982.

Ladybower, Derbyshire In 1945, King George VI opened the Ladybower Reservoir, the result of damming and flooding the Derwent Valley in the Peak District of Derbyshire. Eerily submerging villages and country houses, the resulting 10,000 million gallons of water supply Derby, Sheffield, Nottingham and Leicester.

At the turn of the millennium, Severn Trent Water completed a £23 million refurbishment and restoration of the dam and two road viaducts. This is the Ladybower Viaduct on the A6013 north of Bamford. Much of the original concrete laid onto latticed steel was removed and replaced, the spoil being recycled into new car parks and a visitor centre, and for the repair of cycle ways in the surrounding forests.

private lives In travelling to every corner of England to photograph and write for this book, I have been constantly amazed at the most unlikely places that bridges can be found. This is particularly true of the bridges built for private purposes, ones that we can only cross by invitation.

< **Chantry House, Slapton, Devon** The house and garden were here before the road, so when this winding lane rudely divided them, the little footbridge was built to reunite the two halves. It appears that the garden wants to grow back to reach the house again.

<< **The Island, Newquay, Cornwall** The only privately owned suspension bridge in the country, it is ninety feet long, only three feet wide, and seventy feet above the waves on a Cornish beach. It provides the only access to The Island, and the five-bedroomed house perched on top has the ultimate in sea views. The bridge was built in 1901, and visitors who crossed it to the island include Sir Arthur Conan Doyle whilst a guest of Sir Oliver Joseph Lodge, the inventor of the spark plug.

acknowledgements Many kind people helped me with this book. At Everyman: David Campbell (who said 'Wilton' everytime I saw him), Sandra Pisano and Clémence Jacquinet. At English Heritage: Val Horsler and Simon Bergin. At Anikst Design: Judith Ash and James Warner. For taking the time to help and part with valuable information: G. Laurie at Northumberland County Council, Chris Dixon at Dartford River Crossing Ltd., Thames Europort, PGL Travel's Beam House Activity Centre, Roger Wakerley at Middlesbrough Council, John Stothert, Mr and Mrs Colin Tucker at Wherstead, the 17th Earl of Pembroke at Wilton House, Wiltshire, Rupert Farnsworth for his passion for bridges, and Elizabeth Raven-Hill for everything else.

bibliography *The Ancient Bridges of Mid and Eastern England*, E. Jervoise, The Architectural Press 1932. *George & Robert Stephenson*, L.T.C. Rolt, Penguin Books 1984. *Buildings of England Series*, Penguin Books. *Shell County Guides*, Faber & Faber. *Bridges*, edited by Sir Hugh Casson, Chatto & Windus 1963. *Medieval Bridges*, Martin Cook, Shire Publications 1998. *The Great North Road*, Norman W. Webster, Adams & Dart 1974. *Bridges of Bedfordshire*, Angela Simco & Peter McKeague, Bedfordshire Archaeology Monograph No.2 1997. *London's Secret History*, Peter Bushell, Constable 1983. *Nairn's London*, Ian Nairn, Penguin 1966. *English Cities & Small Towns*, John Betjeman, Collins 1943. *Iron Bridge to Crystal Palace*, Asa Briggs, Thames and Hudson 1979. *Aerofilms Guide to The Thames Path*, Helen Livingstone, Ian Allan 1993

< **Ovingham Bridge, Northumberland** Pier technology on the Tyne at Ovingham. Slender piers and the high roadway allows for all the vagaries of a fast flowing river that can so rapidly increase its depth. In 1828 the coffin of Thomas Bewick, the master wood engraver, was brought here by boat across the Tyne from Cherryburn on its journey to Ovingham church, his final resting place. The 1884 bridge connects the village with Prudhoe and its castle on a wooded hillside above the river.

Overleaf
Duddington, Northamptonshire (see page 17)